Documents of American Democracy

DECLARATION OF INDEPENDENCE

Sarah Machajewski

PowerKiDS press.

New York

Published in 2017 by The Rosen Publishing Group, Inc.
29 East 21st Street, New York, NY 10010

Editor: Katie Kawa
Book Design: Tanya Dellaccio

Photo Credits: Cover (painting) https://commons.wikimedia.org/wiki/File:Declaration_independence.jpg; Cover (document, p.25 https://commons.wikimedia.org/wiki/File:United_States_Declaration_of_Independence.jpg; p. 5 Jurgen Vogt/Getty Images; p. 5 (Thomas Jefferson) https://commons.wikimedia.org/wiki/File:Official_Presidential_portrait_of_Thomas_Jefferson_(by_Rembrandt_Peale,_1800).jpg; p. 7 https://commons.wikimedia.org/wiki/File:Gilbert_Stuart_Williamstown_Portrait_of_George_Washington.jpg; pp. 9 (both),15 (document), 23 (document) Courtesy of Libary of Congress; p. 11 https://commons.wikimedia.org/wiki/File:Flickr_-_USCapitol_-_The_First_Continental_Congress,_1774.jpg; p. 13 https://commons.wikimedia.org/wiki/File:Congress_voting_independence.jpg; p. 13 (Lee Resolution_ https://commons.wikimedia.org/wiki/File:Lee_Resolution.jpg ;p. 15 (painting) https://commons.wikimedia.org/wiki/File:Writing_the_Declaration_of_Independence_1776_cph.3g09904.jpg; p. 17 John Parrot/Stocktrek Images/Getty Images; p. 19 (top) Blend Images - KidStock/Shutterstock.com; p. 19 (bottom) Sanchai Kumar/Shutterstock.com; p. 21 https://commons.wikimedia.org/wiki/File:Allan_Ramsay_-_King_George_III_in_coronation_robes_-_Google_Art_Project.jpg; p. 23 (painting) https://commons.wikimedia.org/wiki/File:Sprit_of_%2776.2.jpeg; p. 25 (background) James Whelan/Shutterstock.com; p. 27 Kean Collection/Getty Images; p. 28 Everett Historical/Shutterstock.com; p. 29 -/AFP/Getty Images.

Library of Congress Cataloging-in-Publication Data

Names: Machajewski, Sarah, author.
Title: Declaration of Independence / Sarah Machajewski.
Description: New York : PowerKids Press, 2016. | Series: Documents of American democracy | Includes index.
Identifiers: LCCN 2016010413 | ISBN 9781499420777 (pbk.) | ISBN 9781499420791 (library bound) | ISBN 9781499420784 (6 pack)
Subjects: LCSH: United States. Declaration of Independence–Juvenile literature. | United States–Politics and government–1775-1783–Juvenile literature.
Classification: LCC KF4506 .M33 2016 | DDC 973.3/13–dc23
LC record available at http://lccn.loc.gov/2016010413

Manufactured in the United States of America

CPSIA Compliance Information: Batch #BS16PK: For Further Information contact Rosen Publishing, New York, New York at 1-800-237-9932

CONTENTS

AMERICAN IDEALS

"Life, Liberty, and the pursuit of Happiness" is a phrase that means something to all Americans. For many, it reflects the rights people feel they deserve as citizens of the United States. For others, it's a statement of the principles our government was created to uphold. However people interpret this phrase, one thing is certain—it's shaped life in the United States since it was written in 1776.

This phrase is part of one of the most memorable lines of the Declaration of Independence. Written over the course of just one month during the American Revolution, this document told the world that the American colonies were no longer subjects of the British king. They were free states with the power to declare their own independence.

People can view the original Declaration of Independence at the National Archives in Washington, D.C., shown here. It's displayed alongside the U.S. Constitution and the Bill of Rights. Together, the three documents are called the "charters of freedom."

THOMAS JEFFERSON

Thomas Jefferson is the person most often associated with the Declaration of Independence. At the age of 33, he wrote the majority of this document. This wasn't his only accomplishment, though. He served as George Washington's first secretary of state, the vice president under John Adams, and the third president of the United States. The ideas Jefferson wrote about in the Declaration of Independence have shaped the government of the United States since it was founded.

THE ROAD TO WAR

Great Britain established its first permanent North American settlement in Jamestown, Virginia, in 1607. By 1733, Britain had 13 permanent colonies in North America. They extended from part of Massachusetts in the North to Georgia in the South. People living in the American colonies were subjects of Great Britain. Colonists had to follow decisions and laws the king and **Parliament** made for them, even though the government was thousands of miles away.

From 1754 to 1763, Britain and its Native American allies fought France and its Native American **allies** in a conflict now known as the French and Indian War. This part of a larger war between the two countries was fought on American soil. American colonists' desire for independence grew stronger after the French and Indian War. The consequences of the war led many colonists to become unhappy with the way Britain treated them.

George Washington, shown here, gained experience as a military leader during the French and Indian War. He became a central figure in the fight for independence and eventually became the first U.S. president.

GROWING RESENTMENT

Britain won the French and Indian War, but it was expensive. The British government felt the colonists should help pay for the war and for the cost of keeping British troops in the colonies for protection. To raise money, Parliament imposed taxes on many kinds of goods—such as stamps, sugar, and tea—without the colonists' consent, or permission. Britain also attempted to keep colonists from moving west into lands acquired after the war.

THE STAMP ACT

*One of Parliament's most **controversial** decisions was the passage of the Stamp Act of 1765. It taxed printed papers and dice in the colonies and limited colonists' right to a trial by jury if they were accused of breaking the law. Many colonists were fiercely opposed to the Stamp Act. Violent protests followed, and tax collectors fled their posts out of fear. In 1765, a group of colonial representatives met for what's now called the Stamp Act Congress and wrote a **petition** to the king. Called the "Declaration of Rights and Grievances," it stated 13 reasons why the acts violated colonists' rights. In 1766, Parliament repealed, or did away with, the Stamp Act, but resentment in the colonies was only growing stronger.*

This political cartoon from the colonial era shows a funeral for the Stamp Act. Political cartoons were one way the colonists expressed their growing resentment.

These actions made many colonists angry. They felt British leaders **violated** their rights as citizens. They resented that the government made decisions without their input. Colonial leaders argued the taxes were illegal since the colonists didn't have proper representation in Parliament. Soon, some colonists began making their anger known. Widespread protests sometimes turned violent, and the relationship between Britain and its colonies became worse.

THE WAR BEGINS

By the 1770s, a growing number of colonists were acting out against British rule. In 1774, Parliament passed the Coercive Acts, which some colonists called the "Intolerable Acts," to tighten Britain's control over its colonies. The acts closed Boston Harbor, required colonists to house British soldiers, and imposed other harsh laws on the colonies.

In September 1774, representatives from 12 of the 13 colonies met to discuss how to address the problems with Britain. This meeting became known as the First Continental Congress. The representatives wrote petitions and letters to the British king, but it soon became clear that the king had no intention of answering them. In April 1775, the first shots of the American Revolution were fired at Lexington and Concord in Massachusetts. The war that would lead to American independence had begun!

A SOURCE OF INSPIRATION

The Declaration and Resolves of the First Continental Congress was written to explain the colonial point of view after the passage of the Intolerable Acts. This document is sometimes called the Declaration of Colonial Rights, and it was modeled after the petition that helped end the Stamp Act almost 10 years earlier. In both documents, the authors list their reasons for writing, address the concerns they have, and state what they want or plan to do. There are many similarities between these documents and the Declaration of Independence.

Shown here is a meeting of the First Continental Congress. This painting can be seen in the U.S. Capitol in Washington, D.C.

A CALL FOR INDEPENDENCE

At first, most colonists didn't see independence as the only option. They simply wanted the rights they were entitled to as subjects of the British Empire.

This view changed as time went on and the fighting continued. Many Americans were also influenced by a **pamphlet** titled *Common Sense*, which was written by Thomas Paine. This popular pamphlet stated independence was the only path for America's future that made sense.

The Second Continental Congress made the first clear move toward independence on June 7, 1776. That day, Richard Henry Lee of Virginia read a resolution before his fellow **delegates**. The three-part resolution called for the **drafting** of a plan for the colonies to unite as a **confederation**, a plan to form partnerships with foreign countries, and a declaration of independence.

The Second Continental Congress didn't vote on the Lee Resolution, shown here, right away. The delegates planned to meet again on July 1. In the meantime, Congress assembled committees to address each part of the Lee Resolution.

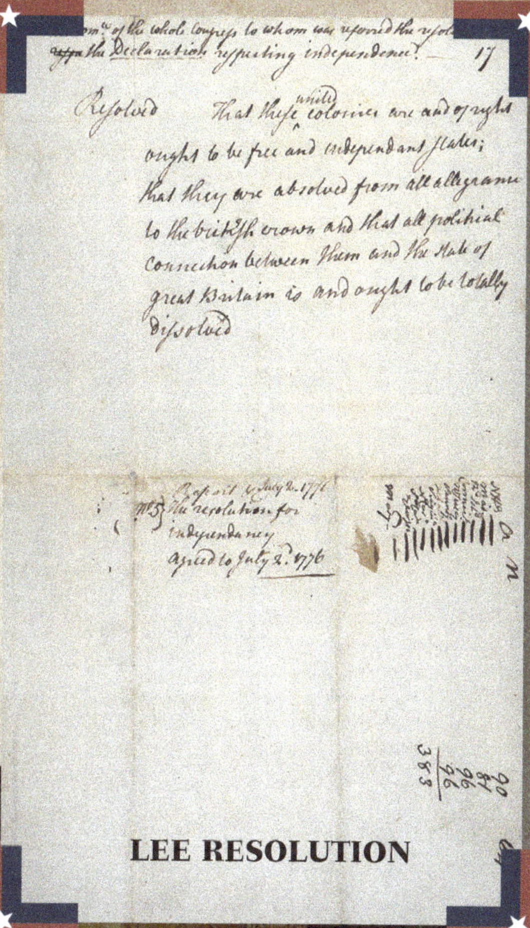

the Declaration respecting independence. 17

Resolved That these united colonies are and of right ought to be free and independant states; that they are absolved from all allegiance to the british crown and that all political connection between them and the state of great Britain is and ought to be totally dissolved

Report of July 2. 1776 the resolution for independancy agreed to July 2d. 1776

LEE RESOLUTION

WRITING HISTORY

Five men were chosen to address the Lee Resolution's call for a declaration of independence. They were Thomas Jefferson, Benjamin Franklin, John Adams, Robert Livingston, and Roger Sherman. These men were to write a document explaining why the colonies wanted to be free from British rule.

Though the committee members discussed ideas together, they chose Jefferson to write the first draft. From June 11 to June 28, 1776, he wrote one of the most important documents in American history.

Jefferson showed early drafts of his writing to Franklin and Adams, who helped him improve it. Then, this committee presented a draft to the Second Continental Congress. The delegates then had a chance to **revise** it. Finally, on July 4, Congress adopted the Declaration of Independence.

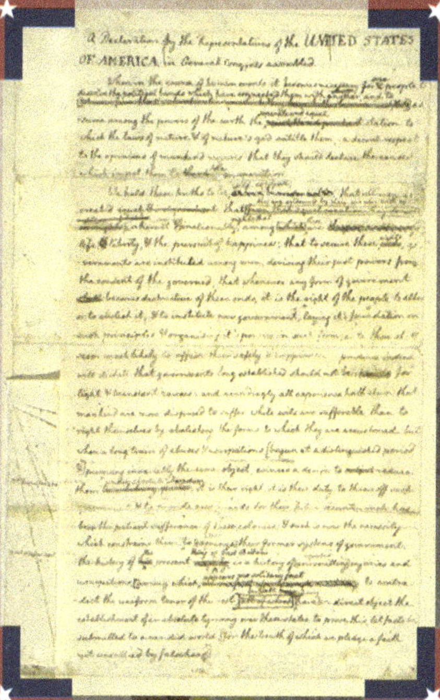
A Declaration by the Representatives of the UNITED STATES OF AMERICA in General Congress assembled.

Pictured here is Jefferson's rough draft of the Declaration of Independence. It's easy to see where he and other members of Congress made changes and crossed out words and sentences.

THE INTRODUCTION

Some historians divide the Declaration of Independence into five parts. The first part is the introduction. It's very short—just one sentence. However, that sentence is long and meaningful.

The introduction justifies why this document was written. It tells the reader it's part of God's law and "the Laws of Nature" for people to want to be politically free. It also states that people should declare the reasons why they want to be free when separating from another country. That's the purpose of this document.

This introduction is powerful because it makes the colonists' cause seem very important. It places the struggle for American independence in the "Course of human events." It's not just a conflict between the colonies and Britain—it's a historical moment that means something for all people.

Historians have pointed out that the language used in the introduction sets the tone for the Declaration of Independence. It doesn't ask readers to join the colonies' cause. Instead, it simply declares that independence is "necessary."

"When in the Course of human events, it becomes necessary for one people to dissolve the political bands which have connected them with another, and to assume among the powers of the earth, the separate and equal station to which the Laws of Nature and of Nature's God entitle them, a decent respect to the opinions of mankind requires that they should declare the causes which impel them to the separation."

THE PREAMBLE

The second part of the Declaration of Independence is called the **preamble**. In this section, the writers state a general philosophy of how a government should serve its people. The text doesn't refer to the British government, the colonial governments, or the conflict between them. Instead, it connects the desire for independence with what the writers saw as universal principles.

The preamble declares that "all men are created equal," and that men have God-given rights that can never be taken away: "Life, Liberty, and the pursuit of Happiness." It goes on to state that people form governments to protect these rights, and the only way a government has power is if the people agree to it. Finally, it states if a government violates these rights and abuses its power, the people have the right to launch a revolution.

The preamble of the Declaration of Independence contains some of the most famous words in American history. This philosophy of government means as much to people today as it did when it was written.

"We hold these truths to be self-evident, that all men are created equal, that they are endowed by their Creator with certain unalienable Rights, that among these are Life, Liberty and the pursuit of Happiness. That to secure these rights, Governments are instituted among Men, deriving their just powers from the consent of the governed."

ADDRESSING THE KING

The Declaration of Independence doesn't directly mention the conflict between the American colonies and the British king until 273 words in. At this point in the document, which is considered the first part of its body, the writers detail 27 things the king did wrong. The writers present these wrongs as a list of facts.

This description of the king's "long Train of Abuses" is the longest part of the Declaration of Independence. The writers accuse the king of taxing colonists without their consent, cutting off trade, taking away the right to a trial by jury, suspending colonial governments, and "destroy[ing] the lives of [the] people."

At the end of the list, the writers claim their petitions have been ignored. This, they argue, is the act of a tyrant.

King George III ruled Britain before, during, and after the American Revolution. He was viewed by many American people—including the writers of the Declaration of Independence—as "unfit to be the ruler of a free people."

"In every stage of these Oppressions We have Petitioned for Redress in the most humble terms: Our repeated Petitions have been answered only by repeated injury. A Prince whose character is thus marked by every act which may define a Tyrant, is unfit to be the ruler of a free people."

WRAPPING IT UP

An address to the British people follows the declaration's list of the king's abuses. This second part of the document's body is directed at the people whose support American leaders tried—and failed—to win. The language used in this part compares the people and the king, because they both ignored the colonists.

The conclusion is the fifth and last part of the Declaration of Independence. The writers had explained all the reasons the American colonies required freedom. In the conclusion, the writers declare the former colonies to now be "Free and Independent States." The conclusion goes on to list the powers these states now have. They include the power to conduct trade and declare war and peace.

Congress approved the Declaration of Independence on July 4, 1776, in Philadelphia, Pennsylvania. Today, we celebrate July 4 as Independence Day—a national holiday!

ANNOUNCING INDEPENDENCE

John Dunlap was the official printer for Congress. On July 4, the committee took a copy of the Declaration of Independence to Dunlap's shop. He printed copies of it overnight, though the exact number is unknown. The next morning, Dunlap's ***broadsides*** *were given to members of Congress to display and give to others as they saw fit. Today, there are 26 copies of his original printing known to exist. In 1989, an original Dunlap broadside was found hidden behind a painting. The painting was purchased at a flea market for only $4, but the hidden broadside was worth millions!*

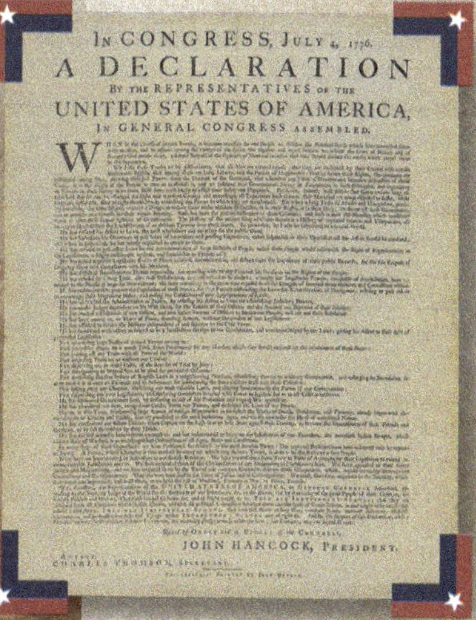

IN CONGRESS, JULY 4, 1776.

A DECLARATION

BY THE REPRESENTATIVES OF THE

UNITED STATES OF AMERICA,

IN GENERAL CONGRESS ASSEMBLED.

JOHN HANCOCK, PRESIDENT.

SIGN HERE

It's commonly thought that all the members of Congress signed the Declaration of Independence on July 4, 1776. However, that didn't happen for almost a month!

New York didn't approve the Declaration of Independence until July 9, and Congress ordered the document to be engrossed on July 19. Engrossing is the process of officially preparing a document in its final form with large, clear writing. Records show the Declaration of Independence was signed on August 2. Some delegates signed later than that, and some didn't sign it at all. There are 56 signatures on the document.

As president of the Second Continental Congress, John Hancock signed first. His signature is the largest, and it's in the middle of the page. The rest of the signatures are organized according to the location of the states they represented—in geographical order from New Hampshire to Georgia.

This is a copy of the Declaration of Independence that was made by William J. Stone in 1823. The original document is too faded to read now, so this version is often the one used.

OFFICIALLY INDEPENDENT

News of the Declaration of Independence spread quickly after it was adopted. Newspapers and broadsides brought the document to the American people. George Washington—the leader of the Continental army at that time—read it out loud to his troops in New York City on July 9, 1776.

The news of American independence also reached Europe. In 1778, the United States formed an alliance with France. This was the first formal recognition of U.S. independence through a treaty with another country. France's troops, ships, and other military support helped the United States win the American Revolution.

However, King George III refused to recognize the states' independence. The battles of the American Revolution continued until 1781, when British forces surrendered at Yorktown, Virginia. The 1783 Treaty of Paris officially ended the war.

By signing the Treaty of Paris, Britain agreed to two important conditions. First, it recognized the United States as an independent nation. Second, it agreed to new territory borders that would give the United States the freedom to expand west.

A LASTING LEGACY

While the Declaration of Independence is one of the United States' most important documents, it doesn't contain completely original ideas. Philosophers had previously written about many of the political ideals reflected in this document. The Declaration of Independence isn't a legal document, and it didn't grant rights to anyone. However, its legacy has endured throughout our nation's history.

Elizabeth Cady Stanton

The Seneca Falls Convention of 1848 modeled its Declaration of Sentiments concerning women's rights after the Declaration of Independence. Abraham Lincoln referred to it in his Gettysburg Address. Martin Luther King Jr. spoke of it in his famous "I Have a Dream" speech in 1963. The Declaration of Independence remains important because it expresses the central principles of American democracy, which matter as much to us today as they did to people in 1776.

Martin Luther King Jr.

Both Martin Luther King Jr. and Elizabeth Cady Stanton—a leader of the Seneca Falls Convention—helped show that the words of the Declaration of Independence need to be applied to all Americans.

10 Fun Facts About the Declaration of Independence

1	*The engrossed copy of the Declaration of Independence is made of parchment—a kind of treated animal skin—and ink.*
2	*The document is 29.75 inches (75.57 cm) tall and 24.25 inches (61.6 cm) wide.*
3	*Congress made 86 changes to Jefferson's draft of the document.*
4	*After George Washington read the Declaration of Independence aloud in New York City, people tore down a statue of King George III. The metal from the statue was used to make musket balls!*
5	*The back of the document reads "Original Declaration of Independence, dated 4th July 1776."*
6	*A mysterious handprint can be found on the original copy of the Declaration of Independence. Historians still don't know whose hand made it.*
7	*The ink on the front of the original document has faded due to poor preservation practices.*
8	*Today, the Declaration of Independence is protected by bulletproof glass.*
9	*Congress declared the Fourth of July as a national holiday in 1870.*
10	*The Declaration of Independence was moved to Fort Knox during World War II for protection.*

GLOSSARY

ally: A person or country associated with another for a common purpose.

broadside: A sheet of paper printed on one side only, forming one large page.

confederation: A league of people or groups united for common interests or goals.

controversial: Likely to give rise to disagreement.

delegate: A person sent to a meeting or convention to represent others.

draft: An early version of a piece of writing. Also, to put something into written form.

pamphlet: A short printed publication with no cover or with a paper cover.

Parliament: The British lawmaking body.

petition: A formal written request to a leader or government regarding a particular cause.

preamble: An introduction that often gives the reasons for the parts that follow.

revise: To change.

violate: To fail to respect someone's rights.

INDEX

WEBSITES

Due to the changing nature of Internet links, PowerKids Press has developed an online list of websites related to the subject of this book. This site is updated regularly. Please use this link to access the list:
www.powerkidslinks.com/amdoc/dec